Over the years, unscientifically collected words of wisdom from some of the greatest thinkers and people builders the world has ever known. It is with great appreciation that I've assembled just some of these ideas. To the best of my knowledge, all quotations included here fall under the fair use or public domain guidlines of copyright law in the United States. If you believe that any quotation violates a copyright you hold or represent, I will immediately remove it upon notification pending good-faith resolution of any dispute.

This 2006 edition is published by People Skills Press. People Skills Press and design are trademarks of People Skills Press.

People Skills Press
P.O. Box 57115
Pleasant Hill, Iowa 50327
www.peoplebuiler.com

Designer: John L. Gearheart

Printed and bound in Logan, Iowa.

Publisher's Cataloging in Publication (PCIP) is available from the publisher by contacting: People Skills Press.
ISBN: 0-9703038-0-7

Contents

Introduction 1

Together We Can 3

Together We Will 65

Together We Did 113

Index to Authors 133

About the Author 135

There is a Proverb that says, "A word aptly spoken is like apples of gold in settings of silver." Someone else or you yourself felt it was important for you to have some "words" that motivate, so here is a book filled with gold and silver.

Teamwork is such an overused word and yet at times it can be underused. It depends on the leader and it depends on the team. I've discovered in my leadership journey that my success is greatly influenced by the kind of people with whom I surround myself.

You've heard it said, "It's lonely at the top!" The reason it is lonely at the top is because people do not take anyone with them. So, TOGETHER WE... says it all. I want to make the journey to the top with as many people as possible. Each step of the way will be a reminder of how blessed I am to have wonderful people and friends in my life. Each detour will be an opportunity for the team to refocus, revisit, and re-establish the mission and the goal. It will become a very unifying experience and one that benefits, not defeats. Each victory will be a time to celebrate and establish a bigger vision or goal that the team will work towards.

When the team succeeds, we'll all remind each other that TOGETHER WE CAN... and looking forward with determination and passion, we'll be reminded that TOGETHER WE WILL... and on top of victory mountain, we'll all be reminded that TOGETHER WE DID.

Wow! Talk about fun. Talk about excitement. Talk about a journey. Use these words as apples of gold in settings of silver. And when someone says you have a "silver tongue," it will be a tremendous compliment because TOGETHER is what made it happen.

The BEST is yet to come. Let's do it together and even though we might not have met, we can travel the road of leadership and teamwork together. Let's start with a few apples.

This book is dedicated to Kim and Dee Wermersen

who live and share a TOGETHER WE CAN

attitude in everything.

And to the 2005-2006 Class of Governors

from Kiwanis International whose leadership proved

TOGETHER WE DID.

together

we can

together, we will

together, we did

Life is a great big canvas;
throw all the paint on it you can.

— Danny Kaye

When you were born, everyone around you was smiling and you were crying. **Live your life** so that when you die, you're smiling and everyone around you is crying.

— Unknown

We are not powerless specks of dust drifting around in the wind, blown by random destiny. We are, each of us, like beautiful snowflakes unique, and born for specific reason and purpose.

— Elizabeth Kubler-Ross

Life is not measured by the number of breaths we take
but by the moments that take our breath away.

— Unknown

Most men pursue pleasure with such breathless haste
that they hurry past it.

— Soren Kierkegaard

The tragedy of life is not that it ends so soon,
but that we wait so long to begin it.

— W.M. Lewis

The best part of life is not just surviving, but thriving with passion and compassion, and humor and style, and generosity and kindness.

— *Maya Angelou*

My interest is in the future, because I am going to spend the rest of my life there.

— *Charles Kettering*

The ultimate test of a man's conscience may be his willingness to sacrifice something today for future generations whose word of thanks will not be heard.

— *Gaylord Nelson*

Let us not look backward in anger
or forward in fear
but around in awareness.

— James Thurber

A person can stand almost anything
except a succession of ordinary days.

— Johann Wolfgang VonGoethe

Anyone who stops learning is old, whether at twenty or eighty.
Anyone who keeps learning stays young.
The greatest thing in life is to keep your mind young.

— *Henry Ford*

Look at everything as though you were
seeing it either for the first or last time.
Then your time on earth will be filled with glory.

— *Betty Smith*

Never tell a young person that anything cannot be done.
God may have been waiting centuries for someone
ignorant enough of the impossible to do that very thing.

— *John Andrew Holmes*

What I like is that young people don't know why not.
Our generation spends too much time telling young
people why their dreams won't work and not enough
time getting out of their way.

— *Unknown*

The most damaging phrase in the English language is:
"It's always been done that way."

— *Grace Murray Hopper*

When you have exhausted all possibilities,
remember this – you haven't.

— *Thomas Edison*

The universe is full of magical things
patiently waiting for our wits
to grow sharper.

— *Eden Phillpotts*

We need a renaissance of wonder. We need to renew, in our hearts and in our souls, the deathless dream, the eternal poetry, the perennial sense that life is miracle and magic.

— *E. Merrill Root*

Let us be a little humble; let us think that the truth may not perhaps be entirely within us.

— *Jawaharlal Nehru*

Discovery consists in seeing what everybody has seen
and thinking what nobody has thought.

— *Albert von Szent-Gyorgyi*

Who was the first person to look at a cow and say
"I think I'll squeeze these dangly things here,
and drink whatever comes out"?

— *Unknown*

Skate to where the puck is going to be,
not where it has already been.

— Wayne Gretzky

Two roads diverged in a wood,
and I, I – took the one less traveled by,
and that has made all the difference.

— Robert Frost

In order to discover new lands, one must be willing
to lose sight of the shore for a very long time.

— Andre Gide

Twenty years from now you will be more
disappointed by the things that you didn't do than
by the ones you did do. So throw off the bowlines.
Sail away from the safe harbor. Catch the trade
winds in your sails. Explore. Dream. Discover.

— Mark Twain

All men dream, but not equally. Those who dream by night in the dusty recesses of their minds wake in the day to find that it was vanity; but the dreamers of the day are dangerous men, for they may act their dream with open eyes, to make it possible.

— *Lawrence of Arabia*

Imagination is the true magic carpet.

— *Norman Vincent Peale*

Imagination is the highest kite one can fly.

— *Lauren Bacall*

Opportunities
are seldom labeled.

— *John A. Shedd*

Opportunity
is missed by most people
because it is dressed in overalls
and looks like hard work.

— *Thomas Edison*

Our real duty is always found running in the direction
of our worthiest desires.

— *Randolph S. Bourne*

The small choices and decisions we make a hundred times
a day add up to determining the kind of world we live in.

— *Harold S. Kushner*

How wonderful it is that nobody need wait a single moment before starting to improve the world.

— *Anne Frank*

Your future depends on many things,
but mostly on you.

— *Frank Tyger*

There is only one real
failure in life that is possible,
and that is not to be true
to the best one knows.

— *John Farrar*

You have two choices in life: You can dissolve into the mainstream or you can be distinct. To be distinct, you must be different. To be different, you must strive to be what no one else but you can be.

— *Alan Ashley-Pitt*

A competitive world has two possibilities for you. You can lose. Or, if you want to win, you can change.

— *Lester C. Thurow*

There are many who are living far below their possibilities because they are continually handing over their individualities to others. Do you want power in the world? Then be yourself. Be true to the highest within your soul and then allow yourself to be governed by no customs or conventionalities or arbitrary man-made rules that are not found on principle.

— *Ralph Waldo Emerson*

Too many people overvalue what they are not
and undervalue what they are.

—— Malcom Forbes

To be a great champion you must believe
you are the best. If you're not, pretend you are.

—— Muhammad Ali

To be a champ you have to believe in yourself
when nobody else will.

—— Sugar Ray Robinson

Most of us die with our music unplayed...
We should try to step out of our comfort
zones and do the things we're capable of.

— Mary Kay Ash

When I stand before God at the end of my life,
I would hope that I would not have a single bit of talent
left and could say, "I used everything you gave me."

— Erma Bombeck

A life without purpose is a languid, drifting thing;
Every day we ought to review our purpose, saying to
ourselves: This day let me make a sound beginning,
for what we have hitherto done is naught!

— *Thomas A. Kempis*

What lies behind us and what lies before us are tiny matters compared to what lies within us.

— *William Morrow*

Man improves himself as he follows his path; if he stands still, waiting to improve before he makes a decision, he'll never move.

— *Paulo Coelho*

None will improve your lot if you yourself do not.

— *Bertolt Brecht*

We are all pencils
in the hand of a writing God
who is sending love letters
to the world.

— Mother Teresa

I believe every day we are sending ourselves
messages about what we need to become –
we need to listen to that voice.

— *Eileen Fisher*

A person is only as big
as the dream they dare to live.

— *Unknown*

To find what you were put here to do
is a complete joy.

— *Unknown*

It's not important what you gather,
it's important what you scatter.

— *Helen Walton*

Throw your heart over the fence
and the rest will follow!

— *Unknown*

As we let our own light shine, we unconsciously give other people permission to do the same. As we are liberated from our own fear, our presence automatically liberates others.

— *Nelson Mandela*

Let no one ever come to you without leaving better and happier.

— *Mother Teresa*

If you want others to be happy,
practice compassion.
If you want to be happy,
practice compassion.

— *Dalai Lama*

Kindness in words creates confidence.
Kindness in thinking creates profoundness.
Kindness in giving creates love.

— *Lao-tzu*

Instead of always harping on man's faults,
tell him of his virtues. Try to pull him out of his
rut of bad habits. Hold up to him his better self, his
real self that can dare and do and win out.

— *Eleanor Porter*

I don't like that man.
I must get to know him better.

— *Abraham Lincoln*

Tolerance and celebration of individual
differences fuel lasting love.

— *Tom Hannah*

For attractive lips, speak words of kindness.

For lovely eyes, seek out the good in people.

For a slim figure, share your food with the hungry.

For beautiful hair, let a child run his or her fingers through it once a day.

For poise, walk with the knowledge that you'll never walk alone.

— *Audrey Hepburn*

Kind words can be short and easy to speak,
but their echoes are truly endless.

— Mother Teresa

Love and kindness are never wasted. They always
make a big difference. They bless the one who
receives them, and they bless you, the giver.

— Barbara DeAngelis

Most of us would rather be ruined by praise
than saved by criticism.

— Norman Vincent Peale

We can't help everyone,
but everyone can help someone.

— *Dr. Loretta Scott*

Do not wait for leaders;
do it alone, person to person.

— *Mother Teresa*

If you wish to be a leader you will be frustrated, for a very few people wish to be led. If you aim to be a servant you will never be frustrated.

— *Frank F. Warren*

An army of sheep led by a lion would defeat an army of lions led by a sheep.

— *Arab Proverb*

As you grow older you will discover that you have two hands. One for helping yourself, and the other for helping others.

— *Abraham Lincoln*

It is a fine thing to have ability, but the ability to discover ability in others is the true test.

— *Elbert Hubbard*

People have a way of becoming what you encourage them to be and what you praise them for; that's real people building.

— *Barb Siemens*

It is the nature of man to rise to greatness if greatness is expected of him.

— *John Steinbeck*

Many people have gone a lot further than they thought they could because someone else thought they could.

— *Unknown*

If you have an apple and I have an apple and we exchange these apples, then you and I will still have one apple. But if you have an idea and I have an idea and we exchange these ideas, then each of us will have two ideas.

— *George Bernard Shaw*

When one teaches, two learn.

— *Robert Half*

The glory of friendship is not the outstretched hand, nor the kindly smile, nor the joy of companionship; it is the spiritual inspiration that comes to one when he discovers that someone else believes in him and is willing to trust him with his friendship.

— *Ralph Waldo Emerson*

To handle yourself, use your head;
to handle others, use your heart.

— Unknown

Three keys to more abundant living:
caring for others, daring for others, sharing with others.

— William A. Ward

Don't fail to ask for help when you need it
or you will deny someone the blessings of helping.

— Kinserdahl

If all my friends were to jump off a bridge, I wouldn't
jump with them. I'd be at the bottom to catch them.

— Unknown

The best way to motivate other people to help you
fulfill your goals is to help them fulfill their goals.

— Deepak Chopra

When we seek to discover the best in others,
we somehow bring out the best in ourselves.

— William A. Ward

In everyone's life, at some time, our inner fire goes out. It is then burst into flames by an encounter with another human being. We should all be thankful for those people who rekindle the inner spirit.

— *Albert Schweitzer*

You cannot hold a torch to light another's path without brightening your own.

— *Steve Siemens*

Those who bring sunshine to the lives of others cannot keep it for themselves.

— *James Matthew Barrie*

There is no exercise better for the heart than reaching down and lifting people up.

— *John Andrew Holmes*

When someone does something good, applaud! You will make two people happy.

— *Samuel Goldwyn*

Coming together is a beginning,
staying together is progress,
but working together is success.

— Henry Ford

Enthusiasm is the best protection in any
situation. Wholeheartedness is contagious.
Give yourself if you wish to get others.

— David Seabury

Enthusiasm is one of life's greatest qualities, but it must be practiced to become a dominant factor in one's life. There is real magic in enthusiasm. It spells the difference between mediocrity and accomplishment.

— *Norman Vincent Peale*

The secret of genius is to carry the spirit of the child into old age, which means never losing your enthusiasm.

— *Aldous Huxley*

Years wrinkle the face, but to give up enthusiasm wrinkles the soul.

— *Watterson Lowell*

Enthusiasm is one of the most powerful engines of success. When you do a thing, do it with all your might. Put your whole soul into it. Stamp it with your own personality. Be active, be energetic, be enthusiastic and faithful, and you will accomplish your objective. Nothing great was ever achieved without enthusiasm.

— *Ralph Waldo Emerson*

Apathy can be overcome by enthusiasm, and enthusiasm can be aroused by two things: first, an idea which takes the real imagination by storm; and second, a definite, intelligible plan for carrying that idea into action.

— *Arnold Toynbee*

We only have this moment, sparkling like a star in our hand...and melting like a snowflake. Let us use it before it is too late.

—— Marie Beynon Ray

We all live in a time of paradox, contradiction, opportunity, and above all change. To the fearful, change is threatening because they worry that things may get worse. To the hopeful, change is encouraging because they feel things may get better. To those who have confidence in themselves, change is a stimulus because they believe one person can make a difference and influence what goes on around them. These people are often the doers and the motivators.

—— Buck Rogers

Our attitudes control our lives.
Attitudes are a secret power
working twenty-four hours
a day, for good or bad. It is
of paramount importance that
we know how to harness and
control this great force.

— *Tom Blandi*

A positive attitude will not solve all your problems,
but it will annoy enough people to make it
worth the effort.

— Herm Albright

Do you know what the greatest test is?
Do you still get excited about what you do
when you get up in the morning?

— David Seabury

Optimism

is essential to achievement and
it is also the foundation of courage
and true progress.

— *Nicholas Murray Butler*

Optimism is the faith that leads to achievement. Nothing can be done without hope and confidence.

— Helen Keller

The world of achievement
has always belonged to the optimist.

— Joseph Campbell

People call me an optimist, but I'm really an
appreciator...When I was six years old and
had scarlet fever, the first of the miracle drugs,
sulfanilamide, saved my life. I'm grateful for
computers and photocopiers...I appreciate
where we've come from.

— Julian Simon

An optimist is someone who believes that a housefly is looking for a way to get out.

— *George Gene Nathan*

An optimist is a man who gets treed by a lion but enjoys the scenery.

— *Walter Winchell*

Optimism is a force multiplier.

— *Colin Powell*

The optimist sees opportunity in every danger; the pessimist sees danger in every opportunity.

— *Winston Churchill*

In the long run the pessimist may be proved right, but the optimist has a better time on the trip.

— *Daniel L. Reardon*

You can say "I can do it"
or you can say, "I can't do it."
Either way you're going to be right.

— Unknown

Be a step ahead of the ones who say,
"Just do it."
Be the one who says,
"I already did it."

— Barb Siemens

No pessimist ever discovered the secrets
of the stars, or sailed to an uncharted land,
or opened a new heaven to the human spirit.

— *Helen Keller*

There is no sadder sight
than a young pessimist.

— *Mark Twain*

Borrow money from pessimists;
they don't expect it back.

— *Unknown*

If you spend your whole life waiting for the storm, you'll never enjoy the sunshine.

— Morris West

A pessimist is one who is seasick on the entire voyage of life.

— Unknown

Worry is a misuse of imagination.

— Dan Zadra

The reason why **worry** kills more people than work is that more people worry than work.

— Robert Frost

A worrier always seems less troubled by what happens today than by what might happen tomorrow.

— Unknown

You pile up enough tomorrows, and you'll find you've collected a lot of empty yesterdays.

— Harold Hill

The time to repair the roof is when the sun is shining.

— John F. Kennedy

together we can

together we will

together we did

A good plan executed right now is far better than a perfect plan executed next week.

— *George S. Patton*

One thought driven home
is better than three left on base.

— *James Liter*

Even if you are on the right track,
you'll get run over if you just sit there.

— *Will Rogers*

Don't put off until tomorrow
what you can do today,
because if you enjoy it today,
you can do it again tomorrow.

— James A. Michener

You might have a heart of gold,
but so does a hard-boiled egg.

— James A. Michener

Sadder than work left unfinished
is work never begun.

— *Unknown*

Procrastination is the art of keeping up with
yesterday and avoiding today.

— *Wayne Dyer*

If procrastinators had a club,
would they ever have a meeting?

— *Unknown*

The cave you fear to enter
holds the treasure you seek.

— Joseph Campbell

If you wait for the perfect moment when all is safe and assured, it may never arrive. Mountains will not be climbed, races won, or lasting happiness achieved.

— *Maurice Chevalier*

In any moment of decision, the best thing you can do is the right thing, the next best thing is the wrong thing, and the worst thing you can do is nothing.

— *Theodore Roosevelt*

When you cannot make up your mind between two evenly balanced courses of action, choose the bolder.

— *W.J. Slim*

together we will 70

Change is the law of life. And those
who look only to the past or the present
are sure to miss the future.

— *John F. Kennedy*

You cannot step twice into the same river,
for other waters are continually flowing in.
Nothing is permanent but change.

— *Heraclitus*

71 together we will

Not everything that is faced can be changed,
but nothing can be changed until it is faced.

— *James Baldwin*

What we need is a flexible plan for an
ever-changing world.

— *Jerry Brown*

When someone is around to make change, the change
machine works perfectly, and when there isn't, it doesn't.

— *Unknown*

The best way to cope with change is to help create it.

— *Robert Dole*

Never doubt that a small group of thoughtful citizens can change the world. Indeed it is the only thing that ever has.

— *Margaret Mead*

The best way out
is always through.

— *Robert Frost*

Only those who will
risk going too far
can possibly find out
how far one can go.

— *T.S. Eliot*

Faith that the thing can be done is essential to any great achievement.

— *Thomas N. Carruther*

You can't climb up to the second floor without a ladder. When you set your aim too high and don't fulfill it, then your enthusiasm turns to bitterness. Try for a goal that's reasonable, and then gradually raise it. That's the only way to get to the top.

— *Emil Zatopek*

Live your life each day as you would climb
a mountain. An occasional glance towards
the summit keeps the goal in mind,
but many beautiful scenes are to be observed
from each new vantage point.

— *Harold B. Melchart*

We have to continually be jumping off cliffs and
developing our wings on the way down.

— *Kurt Vonnegut*

Do not be too timid and squeamish about your actions.
All life is an experiment.

— *Ralph Waldo Emerson*

together we will 76

Each of us will one day be judged by our standard of life, not by our standard of living; by our measure of giving, not by our measure of wealth; by our simple goodness, not by our seeming greatness.

— *William A. Ward*

God looks for growth, not perfection, so our objective is excellence, not perfection.

— *Unknown*

It is better by noble boldness to run the risk of being subject to half the evils we anticipate than to remain in cowardly listlessness for fear of what might happen.

— *Herodotus*

The ultimate measure of a man is not where he stands in moments of comfort and convenience, but where he stands at times of challenge and controversy.

— *Martin Luther King Jr.*

What you do may seem insignificant,
but it's important that you do it.

— *Mahatma Gandhi*

Find reasons to do the important things,
instead of reasons not to do them.
Risk, experiment, and don't forget to
have some fun while you are at it.

— *Ernie J. Zelinski*

Don't bother about genius.
Don't worry about being clever.
Trust to hard work,
perseverance, and determination.

— *Sir Frederick Treves*

The world is not moved only by
the mighty shoves of the heroes,
but also by the aggregate of the
tiny pushes of each honest worker.

— *Helen Keller*

I hear and I forget. I see and I remember.
I do and I understand.

— *Confucius*

It does not matter how slowly you go
so long as you do not stop.

— *Confucius*

No matter our age or where we've been
or what we've been or what we've said and done,
each sunrise is a reminder that we've only just begun.

— *Unknown*

Hard work spotlights the character of the people:
some people turn up their sleeves, some people turn
up their noses, and some don't turn up at all.

— *Sam Ewing*

There is work that is work and there is play that is play;
there is play that is work and work that is play.
And in only one of these lies happiness.

— *Gelett Burgess*

The highest reward for man's toil
is not what he gets for it,
but what he becomes by it.

— *John Ruskin*

If there is one thing upon this earth that mankind
loves and admires better than another,
it is a brave man, it is the man who dares to look
the devil in the face and tell him he is a devil.

— *James A. Garfield*

83 *together we will*

The three great essentials
to achieving anything worthwhile are:
first, hard work,
second, stick-to-it-iveness,
and third, common sense.

— Thomas Edison

All high achievers plan their work and work their
plan, for they are keenly aware that "luck" is most
often being prepared to take advantage of a situation.

— Unknown

The height of your accomplishments will equal the depth of your convictions.

— *William F. Scolavino*

I long to accomplish a great and noble task, but it is my chief duty to accomplish small tasks as if they were great and noble.

— *Helen Keller*

For anything worth having one must pay the price; and the price is always work, patience, love, self-sacrifice – no paper currency, no promises to pay, but the gold of real service.

— *John Burroughs*

Most of the significant contributions that have been made to society have been made by people who are tired.

— Winston Churchill

A professional is someone who can do his best work when he doesn't feel like it.

— Alistair Cooke

Blessed is the individual who is too busy to worry in the daytime, and too sleepy at night.

— Earl Riney

I don't like work...but I like what is in work...the chance to find yourself. Your own reality...for yourself, not for others ... which no other man can ever know.

— *Joseph Conrad*

Our deeds still travel with us from afar, and what we have been makes us what we are.

— *George Eliot*

Nothing is more endangered in the modern world than the powerful combination of hard work toward meaningful goals joined with an exuberant embrace of the present moment.

— Tom Morris

It is wonderful to be in on the creation of something, see it used, and then walk away and smile at it.

— Lady Bird Johnson

There are no shortcuts to any place worth going.

— *Beverly Sills*

It is better to say, "This one thing I do"
than to say, "These forty things I dabble in."

— *Washington Gladden*

Some people itch for success
when they should be scratching for it.

— *Unknown*

It takes less time to do a thing right
than it does to explain why you did it wrong.

— Henry Wadsworth Longfellow

Always do right...
this will gratify some and astonish the rest.

— Mark Twain

Just when you get really good at something,
you won't need to do it anymore.

— Unknown

If a thing is done wrong often enough,
it becomes correct.

— *Unknown*

The 50-50-90 rule: Anytime you have a
50-50 chance of getting something right,
there's a 90% probability you'll get it wrong.

— *Unknown*

Do what is in your heart to be right.
You'll be criticized anyway.

— Eleanor Roosevelt

If a man does his best, **what else is there?**

— George S. Patton

If you don't have the time to do something right,
where are you going to find the time to fix it?

— Stephen King

The important thing in the Olympic games
is not winning but taking part. The essential thing in life
is not conquering but fighting well.

— Baron Pierre de Coubertin

The minute you start talking about
what you're going to do if you lose...you have lost.

— George Shultz

If you have made mistakes...there is always another chance for you...You may have a fresh start any moment you choose, for this thing we call "failure" is not the falling down, but the staying down.

— *Mary Pickford*

The sages do not consider that making no mistakes
is a blessing. They believe, rather, that the great virtue of man
lies in his ability to correct his mistakes and continually
make a new man of himself.

— *Wang Yang-Ming*

The man who makes no mistakes
does not usually make anything.

— *Bishop W.C. Magee*

Experience is the name everyone gives to his mistakes.

— *Woodrow Wilson*

When you stumble, make it part of the dance.

— Unknown

Some mistakes are too much fun to only make once.

— Unknown

Learn from the mistakes of others. You can't live long enough
to make them all yourself.

— Unknown

Failure is the opportunity to begin again, more intelligently.

— Henry Ford

Always remember that striving and struggle precede success, even in the dictionary.

— *Sarah Ban Breathnach*

A small trouble is like a pebble. Hold it too close to your eye and it fills the whole world and puts everything out of focus. Hold it at a proper distance and it can be examined and properly classified. Throw it at your feet and it can be seen in its true setting, just one more tiny bump on the pathway to life.

— *Celia Luce*

The abundant life does not come to those who have had a lot of obstacles removed from their paths by others. It develops from within and is rooted in strong mental and moral fiber.

— *W. M. Lewis*

The gem cannot be polished without friction, nor man perfected without trials.

— *Chinese Proverb*

The one resolution, which was in my mind long before it took
the form of a resolution, is the keynote of my life. It is this,
always to regard as mere impertinences of fate the handicaps
that were placed upon my life almost at the beginning.
I resolved that they should not crush or dwarf my soul, but
rather be made to blossom, like Aaron's rod, with flowers.

— *Helen Keller*

You can tell how big a person is by what it takes to discourage him.
If you are distressed by anything external, the pain is not due to the
thing itself, but to your estimate of it; and this you have the power
to revoke at any moment.

— *Marcus Aurelius Antoninus*

Challenges make you discover things about yourself that you never really knew. They're what make the instrument stretch...what makes you go beyond the norm.

—— Cicely Tyson

I can't go back to yesterday because
I was a different person then.

—— Lewis Carroll

I think I'd like to be remembered as someone who beat the odds through just plain determination... that I persevered. Because I think that being somewhat of a pest to life, constantly plaguing and pursuing, will bring results.

—*Sylvester Stallone*

Patience and perseverance have a magical effect
before which difficulties disappear and obstacles vanish.

— *John Quincy Adams*

When one door of happiness closes, another opens;
but often we look so long at the closed door
that we do not see the one that has been opened for us.

— *Helen Keller*

One of the things I learned the hard way was that it doesn't pay to get discouraged. Keeping busy and making optimism a way of life can restore your faith in yourself.

— Lucille Ball

Don't let life discourage you; everyone who got where he is had to begin where he was.

— Richard L. Evans

I find that it is not the circumstances in which we were placed, but the spirit in which we face them, that constitutes our comfort.

—*Elizabeth T. King*

It's not whether you get knocked down. It's whether you get up again.

— *Vince Lombardi*

The way I see it, if you want to see the rainbow, you gotta put up with the rain.

— *Dolly Parton*

I've missed more than 9,000 shots in my career. I've lost almost 300 games. Twenty-six times, I've been trusted to take the game-winning shot and missed. I've failed over and over and over again in my life. And that is why I succeed.

— *Michael Jordan*

Real heroes are men who fall and fail and are flawed,
but win out in the end because they've stayed true to
their ideals and beliefs and commitments.

— Kevin Costner

Don't let what you cannot do
interfere with what you can do.

— John Wooden

The beauty of the soul shines out
when a man bears with composure
one heavy mischance after another,
not because he does not feel them,
but because he is a man
of high and heroic temper.

— *Aristotle*

Victory is the sweetest
when you've known defeat.

— *Malcom Forbes*

As long as we have goals that are high enough to be
exciting, there is going to be potential for failure.

— *Ed Newman*

Avoiding danger is no safer in the long run than outright
exposure. Life is either a daring adventure, or nothing.

— *Helen Keller*

Become so wrapped up in something
that you forget to be afraid.

— *Lady Bird Johnson*

If you're never scared or embarrassed or hurt,
it means you never take any chances.

— *Julia Sorel*

Many of our fears are tissue paper thin, and a single
courageous step would carry us clear through them.

— *Brendan Francis*

Our fears are always more numerous than our dangers.

— *Seneca*

Pain nourishes courage. You can't be brave if you've only
had wonderful things happen to you.

— *Mary Tyler Moore*

Courage is not limited to the battlefield or to the Indianapolis 500 or bravely catching a thief in your house. The real tests of courage are... the inner tests, like remaining faithful when nobody's looking, like enduring pain when the room is empty, like standing alone when you're misunderstood, like fighting for what is right even when you know you are going to lose.

— *Charles R. Swindoll*

The greatest test of courage on earth
is to bear defeat without losing heart.

— R.G. Ingersoll

We must constantly build dikes of courage
to hold back the flood of fear.

— Martin Luther King, Jr.

Courage is doing what you're afraid to do.
There can be no courage unless you're scared.

— Eddie Rickenbacker

Even on the springboard to success,
you have to bounce a little.

— Unknown

together we can

together we will

together we did

To know that even one life has breathed easier because you have lived. This is to have succeeded.

— *Ralph Waldo Emerson*

I think the purpose of life is to be useful, to be responsible, to be honorable, to be compassionate. It is, after all, to matter: to count, to stand for something, to have made some difference that you lived at all.

— *Leo C. Rosten*

Joy is not in things, it is in us.

— Richard Wagner

Not the owner of my possessions will you be right to call happy; he more rightly deserves the name of happy who knows how to use God's gifts wisely and to put up with rough poverty, and who fears dishonor more than death.

— Horace

Real joy comes not from ease or riches or from the praise of men, but from doing something worthwhile.

— Pierre Corneille

Remember happiness doesn't depend on who you are or
what you have; it depends solely upon what you think.

— *Dale Carnegie*

The happiness of life is made up of minute fractions –
the little, soon-forgotten charities of a kiss or smile,
a kind look or heartfelt compliment.

— *Samuel Taylor Coleridge*

True happiness is not attained through self-gratification,
but through fidelity to a worthy purpose.

— *Helen Keller*

Happiness lies in the joy of achievement
and the thrill of creative effort.

— *Franklin D. Roosevelt*

Life isn't supposed to be an all-or-nothing battle between misery and bliss. Life isn't supposed to be a battle at all. And when it comes to happiness, well, sometimes life is just okay, sometimes it's uncomfortable, sometimes wonderful, sometimes boring, sometimes unpleasant. When your days are not perfect, it's not a failure or terrible loss. It's just another day.

— *Barbara Sher*

It is only possible to live happily ever after on a day-to-day basis.

— *Margaret Bonnano*

Happiness is nothing more
than good health and bad memory.

— *Albert Schweitzer*

The **healthiest** people are often
those who laugh at themselves. No wonder
laughter is the best medicine.

— *Unknown*

Always **laugh** when you can.
It is cheap medicine.

— *Lord Byron*

Happiness never decreases by being shared.

— *Buddha*

The cheerful live longest in years
and afterwards in our regards.
Cheerfulness is the offshoot of goodness.

— *Christian N. Bovee*

I am happy and content
because I think I am.

— *Alain-Rene Lesage*

There are souls in this world that have the gift of finding joy everywhere and of leaving it behind them when they go.

— Frederick William Faber

The best portion of a good man's life is his little, nameless, unremembered acts of kindness and love.

— William Wordsworth

Truly successful people in life
are givers and forgivers.

— *Unknown*

If you have not often felt the joy of doing a kind act,
you have neglected much, and most of all yourself.

— *A. Neilen*

The manner in which it is given
is worth more than the gift.

— *Pierre Corneille*

Things turn out best for those who make the best
of how things turn out.

— *Art Linkletter*

Of course there is no formula for success except, perhaps,
an unconditional acceptance of life and what it brings.

— *Arthur Rubinstein*

Everything is okay in the end.
If it's not okay, then it's not the end.

— *Unknown*

I honestly think it is better
to be a failure at something
you love than to be a success
at something you hate.

— *George Burns*

Success in life comes not from holding a good hand,
but in playing a poor hand well.

— *Denis Waitley*

Success is going from failure to failure
without loss of enthusiasm.

— *Winston Churchill*

Success is getting what you want;
happiness is wanting what you get.

— *Ingrid Bergman*

Success is determined not by
what you get for reaching your destination,
but by what you become by reaching it.

— Zig Ziglar

Try not to become a man of success.
Rather become a man of value.

— Albert Einstein

No one ever attains very eminent success
by simply doing what is required of him;
it is the amount over and above the required
that determines greatness.

— *Charles Kendall Adams*

Success usually comes to those who
are too busy to be looking for it.

— *Henry David Thoreau*

The reason so few people are successful
is no one has yet found a way
for someone to sit down and slide uphill.

— *W. Clement Stone*

It's kind of fun to do the impossible.

— *Walt Disney*

The height of your accomplishments
will equal the depth of your convictions.

— *William F. Scolavino*

The greatest use of life is to spend it
for something that will outlast it.

— *William James*

Life is what we make it,
always has been,
always will be.

— *Grandma Moses*

How far you successfully go in life
depends on your being tender with the
young, compassionate with the aged,
sympathetic with the striving, and tolerant
of the weak and strong. Because someday
in life you will have been all of these.

— *George Washington Carver*

Index to Authors

A

Adams, Charles Kendall 128
Adams, John Quincy 102
Albright, Herm 52
Ali, Muhammad 24
Angelou, Maya 7
Antonius, Marcus Aurelius.............. 99
Aristotle 107
Ash, Mary Kay................................ 25
Ashley-Pitt, Alan............................. 22

B

Bacall, Lauren 17
Baldwin, James............................... 72
Ball, Lucille...................................103
Barrie, James Matthew.................... 44
Bergman, Ingrid 126
Blandi, Tom.................................... 43
Bombeck, Erma 25
Bonnano, Margaret........................118
Bourne, Randolph S. 19
Bovee, Christian N. 120
Breathnach, Sarah Ban 97
Brecht, Bertolt 27
Brown, Jerry 72
Buddha 120
Burgess, Gelett 82
Burns, George 125
Burroughs, John 85
Butler, Nicholas Murray.................. 53

C

Campbell, Joseph 55,69
Carruther, Thomas N. 75
Carnegie, Dale 116
Carroll, Lewis................................100
Carver, George Washington...........132
Chevalier, Maurice 70
Chopra, Deepak 43
Churchill, Winston 57, 86, 126
Coelho, Paulo................................. 27
Coleridge, Samuel Taylor...............116

Confucius 81
Conrad, Joseph 87
Cooke, Alistair 86
Corneille, Pierre.................... 113, 123
Costner, Kevin...............................106

D

Dalai Lama 32
De Angelis, Barbara 35
de Coubertin, Baron Pierre.............. 93
Disney, Walt 129
Dole, Robert 72
Dyer, Wayne 68

E

Edison, Thomas 11, 18, 84
Einstein, Albert 127
Eliot, George.................................. 74
Eliot, T.S....................................... 74
Emerson, Ralph Waldo........ 23, 41, 48,
73, 109
Evans, Richard L. 103
Ewing, Sam.................................... 82

F

Faber, Frederick William 122
Farrar, John 21
Fisher, Eileen 29
Forbes, Malcom 24, 107
Ford, Henry 9, 46, 96
Francis, Brendan 109
Frank, Ann 20
Frost, Robert 15, 63, 74

G

Gandhi, Mahatma............................ 78
Garfield, James A. 83
Gide, Andre....................................16
Gladden, Washington 89
Goldwyn, Samuel 45
Grandma Moses.............................131
Gretzky, Wayne 15

H

Half, Robert.................................... 40
Hannah, Tom 33
Hepburn, Audrey 34
Heraclitus....................................... 71
Herodotus...................................... 78
Hill, Harold 64
Holmes, John Andrew 10, 45
Hopper, Grace Murray 11
Horace 115
Hubbard, Elbert 38
Huxley, Aldous 47

I

Ingersoll, R.G................................111

J

James, Williams 130
Johnson, Lady Bird...................88, 108
Jordan, Michael 107

K

Kaye, Danny 4
Keller, Helen 55, 60, 80, 85, 99, 102,
108, 115
Kempis, Thomas A........................... 26
Kennedy, John F. 64, 71
Kettering, Charles F. 7
Kierkegaard, Soren............................ 6
King, Elizabeth T. 104
King, Jr., Martin Luther............. 78, 111
King , Stephen 92
Kinserdahl 42
Kubler-Ross, Elizabeth........................ 5
Kushner, Harold S. 19

L

Lao-tzu 29
Lawrence of Arabia 147
Lesage, Alain-Rene 121
Lewis, W.M................................. 6, 98
Lincoln, Abraham 33, 37

Linkletter, Art 124
Liter, James 66
Lombardi, Vincent............................104
Longfellow, Henry Wadsworth 90
Lord Byron... 119
Lowell, Watterson 47
Luce, Celia 98

M

Magee, Bishop W.C. 95
Mandela, Nelson 31
Mead, Margaret 73
Melchart, Harold B. 76
Michener, James A. 67
Moore, Mary Tyler 109
Morris, Tom 88
Morrow, William............................... 27
Mother Teresa 28, 31, 35, 36

N

Nathan, George Jean........................ 56
Nehru, Jawaharlal 13
Neilen, A. 123
Nelson, Gaylord 7
Newman, Ed.....................................108

O

P

Parton, Dolly 104
Patton, George S. 65, 92
Peale, Norman Vincent 17, 35, 47
Phillpotts, Eden................................. 12
Pickford, Mary 94
Porter, Eleanor 33
Powell, Colin..................................... 56
Proverb (Arab)................................... 37
Proverb (Chinese).............................. 98

Q

R

Ray, Marie Benyon........................... 50
Reardon, Daniel L............................. 58
Rickenbacker, Eddie.......................112
Riney, Earl 85
Robinson, Sugar Ray 23
Rogers, Buck..................................... 50
Rogers, Will 66
Roosevelt, Eleanor 92
Roosevelt, Franklin D.....................117
Roosevelt, Theodore......................... 70
Root, E. Merrill 13
Rosten, Leo C. 112
Rubinstein, Arthur 124
Ruskin, John 83

S

Schweitzer, Albert....................44, 119
Scolavino, William F. 85, 130
Scott, Dr. Loretta.............................. 33
Seabury, David 46, 52
Seneca, Lucius Annaeus...................109
Shaw, George Bernard 40
Shedd, John 18
Sher, Barbara 118
Shultz, George 93
Siemens, Barb 38, 59
Siemens, Steve 44
Sills, Beverly 89
Simon, Julian 55
Slim, W.J... 70
Smith, Betty 9
Sorel, Julia 109
Stallone, Sylvester............................. 71
Steinbeck, John................................. 39
Stone, W. Clement 129
Swindoll, Charles R. 110

T

Thoreau, Henry David 128
Thurber, James 8
Thurow, Lester C............................... 22

Toynbee, Arnold J. 49
Treves, Sir Frederick 79
Twain, Mark........................16, 60, 90
Tyger, Frank 21
Tyson Cicely 100

U

Unknown 5, 6, 10, 14, 29, 30,
39, 42, 59, 62, 64, 67, 68, 72, 77, 82,
84, 89, 91, 96, 100, 111, 119, 123, 124

V

von Goethe, Johann Wolfgang 8
Vonnegut, Kurt................................. 76
Von Szent-Gyorgyi, Albert.................14

W

Wagner, Richard 115
Waitley, Denis 126
Walton, Helen 30
Ward, William A. 42, 43, 77
Warren, Frank F.................................. 37
West, Morris 62
Wilson, Woodrow 95
Winchell, Walter................................ 56
Wooden, John..................................107
Wordsworth, William....................122

X

Y

Yang-Ming, Wang 95

Z

Zadra, Dan 63
Zatopek, Emil 75
Zelinski, Ernie J.................................. 79
Ziglar, Zig..127

About the Authors

Steve Siemens is known as Mr. People Builder and Your Balcony Person. He is the founder and president of Siemens People Builders in Des Moines, Iowa.

Steve delights hundreds of audiences nationally and internationally each year. His current clients range from small businesses to Fortune 500 companies and his messages motivate people to action in all walks of life.

Steve earned the status of Certified Speaking Professional (CSP) from the National Speakers Association in 2000. This award recognizes a demonstrated commitment to the speaking profession through proven speaking experience, ongoing education, and ethical behavior. Only 8 percent of speakers worldwide have passed the rigorous criteria to attain the CSP.

Community service is an essential part of Steve's life. He is President of Kiwanis International and will serve in this position through September 30, 2006. Steve is also a member of the Board of Governors for the Iowa Easter Seals and has served as Chairman of the Iowa Board of the Fellowship of Christian Athletes.

Steve and his wife, Barb, live just east of Des Moines in the country. They have an exceptional marriage, three wonderful children, great sons-in-law, and unbelievable grandchildren. What a wonderful fit for a Marriage Encounter group!